A DAY in the LIFE OF...

A BUS DRIVER

Written by Alex Hall

Enslow PUBLISHING

Published in 2025 by Enslow Publishing, LLC
2544 Clinton Street
Buffalo, NY 14224

Written by:
Alex Hall

Edited by:
Rebecca Phillips-Bartlett

Designed by:
Amelia Harris

Cataloging-in-Publication Data

Names: Hall, Alex.
Title: A bus driver / Alex Hall.
Description: Buffalo, NY : Enslow Publishing, 2025. | Series: A day in the life of… | Includes glossary and index.
Identifiers: ISBN 9781978541801 (pbk.) | ISBN 9781978541818 (library bound) | ISBN 9781978541825 (ebook)
Subjects: LCSH: Bus drivers--Juvenile literature. | Bus driving--Juvenile literature.
Classification: LCC HD8039.M8 H355 2025 | DDC 388.3'22023--dc23

Manufactured in the United States of America

CPSIA compliance information: Batch #CW25ENS: For further information contact Enslow Publishing LLC at 1-800-398-2504.

Please visit our website, www.enslowpublishing.com. For a free color catalog of all our high-quality books, call toll free 1-800-398-2504 or fax 1-877-980-4454.

Find us on

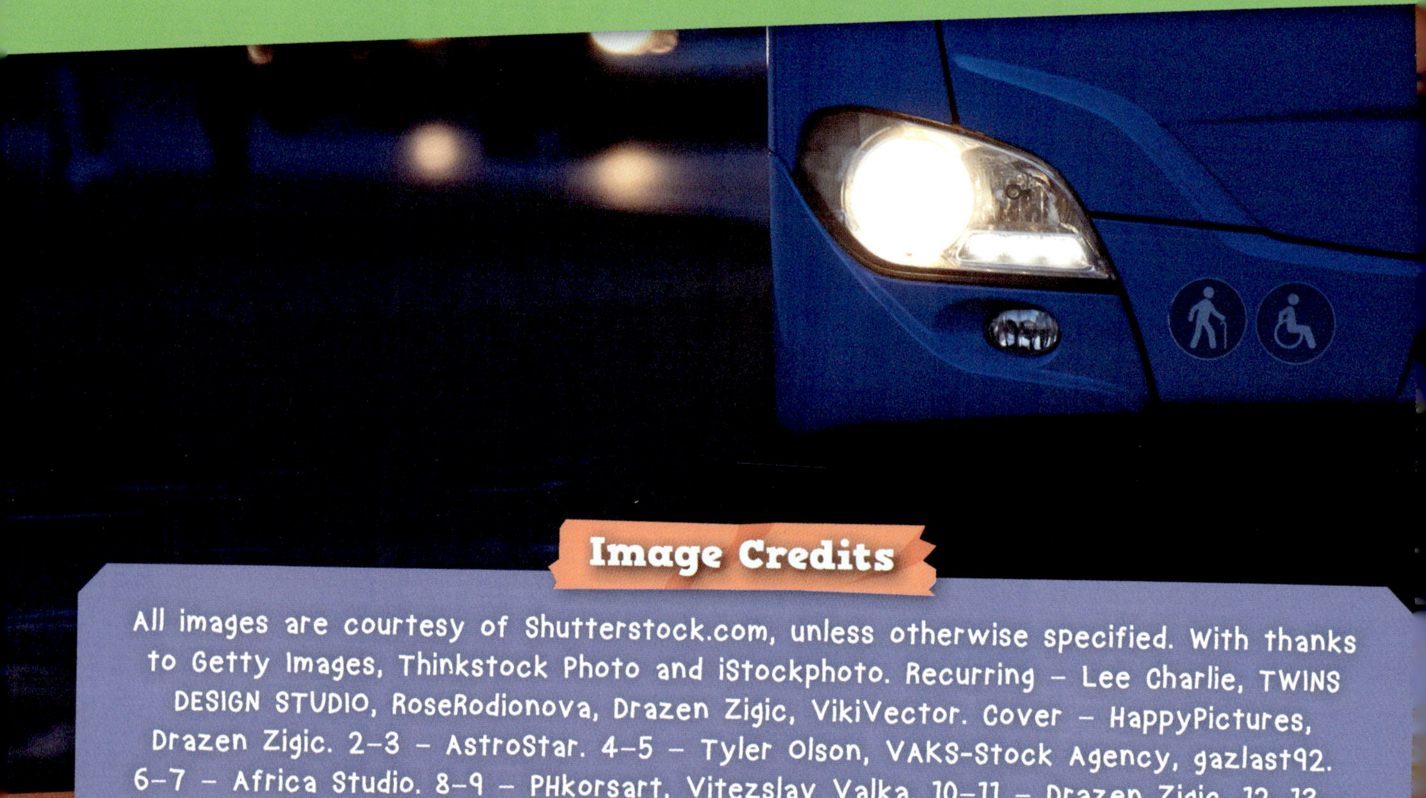

Image Credits

All images are courtesy of Shutterstock.com, unless otherwise specified. With thanks to Getty Images, Thinkstock Photo and iStockphoto. Recurring – Lee Charlie, TWINS DESIGN STUDIO, RoseRodionova, Drazen Zigic, VikiVector. Cover – HappyPictures, Drazen Zigic. 2–3 – AstroStar. 4–5 – Tyler Olson, VAKS-Stock Agency, gazlast92. 6–7 – Africa Studio. 8–9 – PHkorsart, Vitezslav Valka. 10–11 – Drazen Zigic. 12–13 – marat marihal. 14–15 – Inside Creative House, HappyPictures. 16–17 – AstroStar. 18–19 – icon99. 20–21 – Purple Anvil. 22–23 – HappyPictures.

CONTENTS

Words that look like this can be found in the glossary on page 24.

A DAY IN THE LIFE

There are a lot of different jobs that you could do when you grow up. Whether you want to work on your own or in a team, there are lots of jobs to choose from.

Many jobs need people to be good at certain things. Bus drivers are good at driving. They drive many people to different places, such as to schools, around towns, or on long trips.

STARTING THE DAY

Many bus drivers need to get up early in the morning. They might drive a school bus to take children to school, or they may have a morning route around the city.

Some bus drivers keep their bus at their house, but most bus drivers collect their bus from a bus station. Then they check their route plan so they know where they are going.

CHECKING THE BUS

Bus drivers must inspect the entire bus before starting any journeys. They must check the lights, tire pressure, and brakes. This makes sure the bus is safe to drive.

Tire pressure is a measurement of how much air is inside the tire.

Bus drivers must also check whether it is safe enough to drive. Heavy snow or a lot of ice could be very dangerous to the driver and the passengers.

GREETING PASSENGERS

Every bus driver must make sure their passengers pay as they get on the bus. Bus drivers sometimes use math to check that the passengers have paid correctly.

Bus drivers must have people skills as they will often talk to their passengers and greet them. Some passengers ask for directions when they leave the bus. The driver will use their knowledge to help.

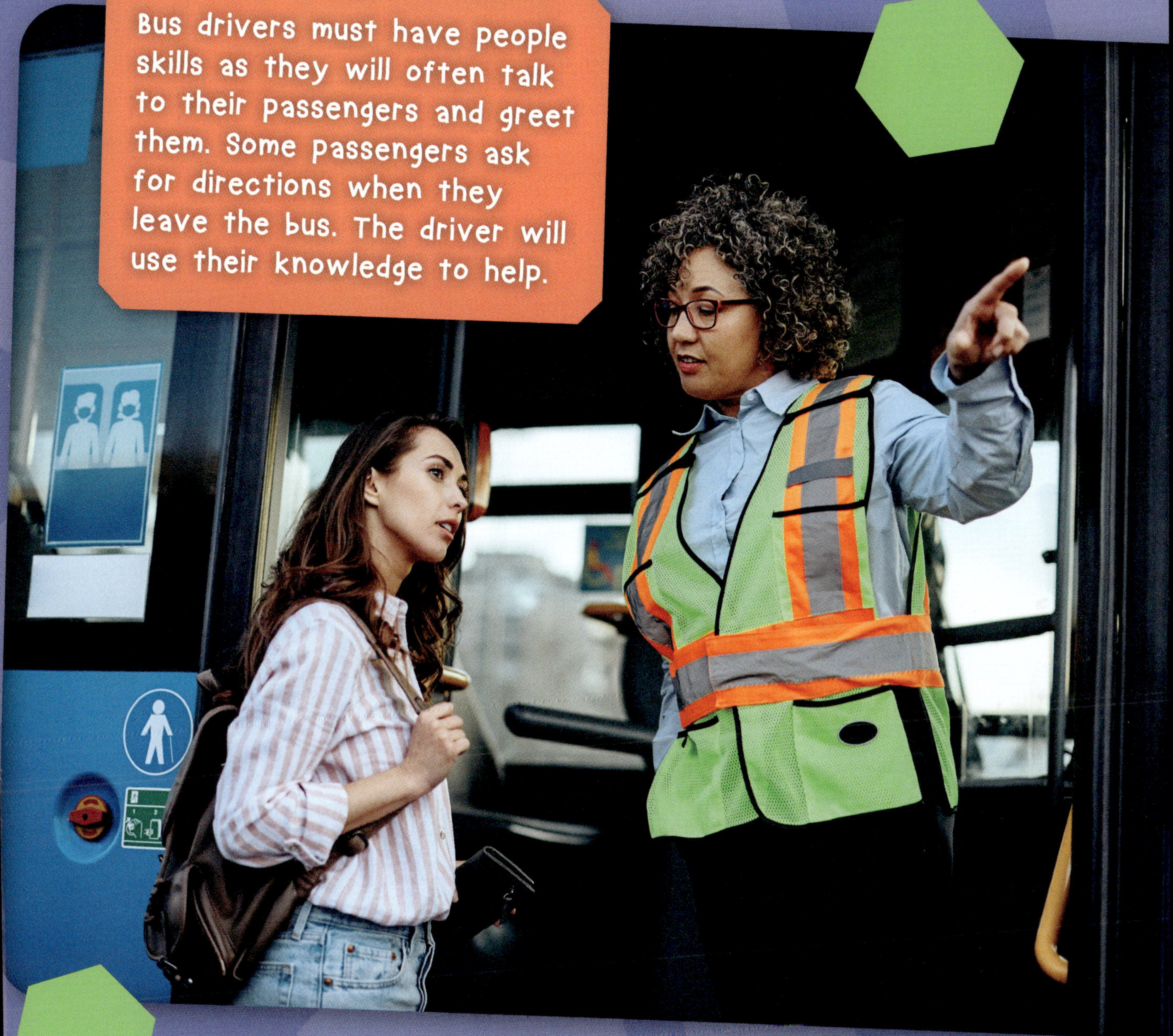

DRIVING CAREFULLY

Bus drivers need to drive carefully all the time. Buses carry a lot of people at once. Some school buses carry up to 90 passengers. That is a lot of people to keep safe.

Bus drivers need to look out for other vehicles, cyclists, and people crossing the road. They need to concentrate to do this. It is important that people riding the bus do not distract the driver.

Bus drivers use side mirrors to see around the bus.

THE BUS ROUTES

Driving to and from different schools or bus stops is the main task of a bus driver. Bus drivers will use their route plan to know where they need to pick up passengers.

Some routes may be short and only take the morning to complete. These routes are usually between bus stops in a small area. However, some routes may be longer and could take the whole day.

LONG JOURNEYS

Some bus drivers will go on very long journeys that can take all day. These journeys could even go to different cities or parts of a country. Sometimes, the journey will continue overnight.

Have you ever been on a long bus journey?

It is important that bus drivers take regular breaks when they are on long trips. This makes sure they stay awake and able to focus properly on driving. It helps to keep everyone safe.

RESPONSIBILITY

Bus drivers have a lot of responsibility. The bus driver must keep their passengers safe even when the bus is not moving. They know how to spot dangers to their passengers.

Many different people ride buses. Sometimes, a passenger may cause trouble. The bus driver will need to use their people skills to solve the problem and keep everyone safe and happy.

How should a good passenger behave?

RETURNING THE BUS

Bus drivers will take their bus back to the bus station or back home when their shift ends. They will then clean the bus so it is ready for the next journey.

Bus drivers may also do paperwork about where they went during the day. It will often be the last task they do. It is useful for bus drivers to have good literacy skills.

WOULD YOU LIKE TO BE A BUS DRIVER?

Bus drivers need to be good at driving to keep the passengers safe. They get to see a lot of different places and meet lots of interesting people on their journeys.

Bus drivers need many important skills and qualifications. They would not be able to do their job without these skills.

Would you like to be a bus driver?

GLOSSARY

INSPECT	to look carefully at something
LITERACY	the ability to read and write
QUALIFICATIONS	proof that someone has trained in a particular skill or to do a particular job
RESPONSIBILITY	to be in charge of doing certain things
ROUTE	the path that is taken to a certain place
SHIFT	the set amount of time that a group works for before handing over to another group to do the same job
VEHICLES	machines that have an engine and are used to carry people or things, such as cars and trucks

INDEX